The New Retirement Basics

The Quick and Easy Guide to Social Security and Medicare

2016

Dr. Donna Davis

Publisher's Note

The author and publisher have made every effort to ensure that the information in this book was correct at press time. The author and publisher do not assume and hereby disclaim any liability to any party for any loss, damage, or disruption by errors or omissions, whether such errors or omissions result from negligence, accident, or any other cause. Further, the author or publisher does not have any control over and does not assume responsibility for author or third-party websites or their content. This book is not intended as a substitute for medical advice of physicians or other trained medical professionals.

Third Printing 2015
Golden Goddess Press
PO Box 6928
Snowmass Village, CO 81615
www.boomerblasts.com

Acknowledgement

To Ronald Reagan for debunking the #1 myth about Social Security.

"Social Security has nothing to do with the deficit. Social Security is totally funded by the payroll tax levied on employer and employee.

If you reduce the outgo of Social Security that money would not go into the General Fund to reduce the deficit. It would go into the Social Security Trust Fund.

So, Social Security has nothing to do with balancing a budget or erasing or lowering the deficit."

—Ronald Reagan

http://ow.ly/VJLRH

Also by Donna Davis
Retirement Basics: Help for Broke Baby Boomers

TABLE OF CONTENTS

Introduction

Ignorance hurts. Don't let it cost you. Make the most of your benefits.

Retirement can be a confusing time. The rules and regulations of Social Security and Medicare can be mystifying, and to top it off, policies have recently changed. The new rules of the Bipartisan Budget Act of 2015 have wide-reaching effects that may pertain to you.

After I wrote my first book, I found that many people were concerned about how Social Security and Medicare programs affected them. This book is a guide that simplifies the basic rules and regulations and answers the most common questions. The information is presented in down-to-earth language that is easy to understand.

The Bipartisan Budget Act of 2015 has changed regulations that affect long-term planning for many retirees. For some the results are devastating and will cause a loss of tens of thousands of dollars.

Many individuals already collecting Social Security will not be affected and will continue receiving payments. For those not yet collecting, the date of your birth will determine whether these strategies are available to you.

This book covers the basics of the new regulations as well as these topics:

- How do the new rules affect me?
- What will Medicare cost now?
- When should I begin collecting Social Security?
- How much will my payments be?
- Can I work and collect Social Security?
- Does Medicare cover all of my medical expenses?

Whether retirement is in your near or distant future, this book helps relieve the stress and anxiety that comes from not knowing how it works. It will give you the foundation to understand the big picture and have confidence in the future. Ignorance hurts. Be informed and learn to make good choices for yourself.

Social Security

Social Security is the nation's insurance program that provides income to older and disabled workers. It insures that U.S. citizens and legal residents who have worked in our country have income later on in life or if they become disabled. In order to be eligible for Social Security Retirement or Disability Insurance, you must be a citizen or legal resident and have worked a minimum of 10 years. Illegal residents do not qualify for or receive Retirement or Disability Insurance.

Social Security is not part of the national budget or the national debt. It is a completely autonomous program. If Social Security benefits were cut, none of that money would go to offset the national deficit. It would go back into the Social Security Fund, which currently has a $2.8 trillion surplus. By law this money can only be used for Social Security.

Social Security is completely funded by payroll tax, interest earned on investments, and tax collected on paid Social Security benefits. None of its funding comes from the Federal General Fund. Financially, it is a completely stand-alone program. Social Security was created after the Depression to provide income to those who have worked regardless of the economic climate of our nation.

You pay 6.2% of your salary to Social Security via payroll tax and your employer pays the same. The money is then divided into two funds. The Old Age and Suvivors Insurance Trust Fund (OASI) and the Disability Insurance Trust Fund (DI). The percentage that goes into each fund varies depending on the demographics of the population. Currently 3.83% goes to the Retirement Fund and 2.37% goes to the Disability Fund. It takes an Act of Congress to adjust the amount allocated to each fund. A change occurred recently with The Bipartisan Budget Act of 2015.

Social Security is not a handout. It's not public assistance or welfare. It is a reflection of the contributions you paid through taxes. The amount you paid in determines the amount you receive. You should never feel guilty or badly about collecting it. You've paid for it your entire working life.

There is a lot of confusion about the basic rules and regulations of Social Security. This can cause you to make decisions that may not be best for you. You may have tried to navigate government websites, or read articles, yet you come away baffled. This chapter will clear up some of the misconceptions and incorrect information. Mistakes with Social Security can be permanent and cost you dearly. Understanding the basics will help you make decisions that will better serve you.

Are You Eligible?

- To be eligible to receive Social Security benefits, you must have earned at least 40 credits.

- You receive one credit for every $1,220 you earn by working.
- The most credits you can earn in a year are four.
- You must have four credits for at least 10 years to earn 40 credits. This makes you eligible for the *minimum* Social Security payment.

Having 40 credits makes you eligible for Social Security, but the amount you earn determines what your monthly payment will be.

- In general, the more you earn, the higher your monthly payment will be.
- The highest payment amount at Full Retirement Age (FRA) is $2,663.
- The maximum income taxed is $118,500 per year, after that amount you no longer pay Social Security tax on additional income.

What is Your Full Retirement Age (FRA)?

Your FRA is the key to determining when you are eligible for benefits and how much your payments will be. It is the age that the Social Security Administration deems you eligible for your "full benefit." FRA used to be 65 for everybody. Now it depends on the year you were born. If you were born 1943–1954 your FRA is 66. For every year over 1954 you add two months. If you were born in 1955 your

FRA is 66 and 2 months. If you were born 1960 or after, your FRA is 67.

Once you know your FRA, you can consider the best time to apply for benefits.

When Can You Apply?

- You can apply for Social Security anytime between the ages of 62 and 70.
- The earliest you can apply is 62, and since there isn't any increase in benefit after age 70, there is no point in waiting any longer.
- When you apply *before* your FRA, your payment will be *reduced*. If you apply *after* your FRA, your payment will be *increased*.

To clarify, FRA is when you are eligible for what is considered your "normal" payment. Any time you apply before your FRA you get less. Any time after FRA, up until age 70, you get more.

These adjustments to your payments are generally permanent. (If you change your mind, you can withdraw your application within 12 months, but you will have to return the total amount of payments you received.) Therefore, deciding when to apply will be the biggest decision you make regarding Social Security. Your choice affects your monthly payment amount for the rest of your life.

Age	% Decreased
62	30
63	25
64	20
65	13.3
66	6.7

Age	% Increased
67	8
68	16
69	24
70	32

For example, if your monthly payment amount at FRA would be $2,000, at 62 your payment would go down to $1,400 for life. If you wait until age 70, your payment amount would go up to $2,600 for life. That's an increase of $1,200 a month by waiting those eight years.

The Best Time for You to Apply

Financial planners and advisors highly recommend that you wait until age 70 to collect so that you will get the highest payment amount when you are older. It's also worth considering that if you did begin collecting at age 62, over the eight years between age 62 and 70 you will have received more than $160,000 in payments. (Based on $2,000 monthly payment amount at FRA.)

The breakeven point between collecting at 62 and 70 is about 80 years old. *You must reach at least 80 to make waiting until 70 pay off.* The average lifespan is 83, but the odds of reaching 90 continue to increase.

How do you decide? One of the biggest factors in determining when to apply for Social Security is something you can't know: How long will you live? Or, How long do you need to provide for yourself?

How Long Will You Live?

Longevity is the wild card when figuring out the best time to apply for benefits.

More people are living into their 90s. What is the likelihood of that for you? You need to estimate how long your money needs to last.

Aside from age and gender, consider how long your family members live. Do your relatives generally live into their 80s or 90s? Is there family history of major illnesses? This may reflect on your lifespan, too.

What is your personal history? Have you suffered major illnesses, serious accidents, or had surgeries? Do you take care of yourself? Did you drink or smoke? Are you overweight? Active?

All of these factors help determine your lifespan and therefore, your ideal time to begin collecting Social Security. There's no way to know for sure how long you're going to live. You can only look at the whole picture and make your best guess.

Summary

- You need 40 credits to be eligible for Social Security benefits.
- Your FRA is when Social Security deems you are eligible for your "full benefit."
- You can apply for Social Security benefits anytime between the ages of 62 and 70.
- If you apply before your FRA, your monthly payment amount will be reduced.
- If you apply after your FRA, your monthly payment will be increased until you reach age 70.
- Longevity is a critical factor in determining the best time for you to apply for Social Security benefits.

Bulk Payments

The New Budget Act (The Bipartisan Budget Act of 2015) has eliminated the Bulk Payment option for anyone born May 1, 1950 or after. Those born before that date are still able to receive a bulk payment for past benefits.

Here's how it works. If you do not begin collecting benefits at your FRA in order to increase your payment amount and then change your mind before age 70, you could get a bulk payment for the amount you missed between your FRA and the current date. If you do this, you will forfeit the 8% per year increase in the monthly payment you would have received by waiting, but you do collect any monies you missed since age 66. This was especially helpful to those who developed severe illnesses or had major life changes after their FRA, enabling them to recoup any monies lost during that time.

How Is Your Benefit Calculated?

To calculate your benefit, the Social Security Administration:

- takes your 35 highest earning years,
- converts them to today's dollars,
- puts the result into a formula and,
- determines your benefit amount.

What Will Your Monthly Payment Be?

You can determine your approximate monthly payment amount at this point in your life and estimate future payments by:

- going online to SSA.gov,
- opening your "My Social Security" account,
- requesting your earning statement,
- using the benefit estimator.

On your statement, you will see your entire lifetime working history and an estimate of your monthly payment, should you keep working and earning a similar amount until your FRA.

You can use the benefit estimator and enter different earning amounts and different ages. You'll be able to see what the difference in your payments would be if you (1.) continued to work until FRA, (2.) applied at age 62, or (3.) waited until age 70 to collect. This gives you a concrete look at the consequences of each option.

If you don't have access to a computer or don't want to open an account, you can order your Social Security Statement over the telephone via an automated system and it will be mailed to you. Call 1-800-772-1213.

Can You Work And Collect Social Security?

Yes, you can. If you have reached your FRA, you can work and earn as much as you can without penalty and still collect your full monthly payment. If you are *under* your FRA, however, there is a penalty for anything you earn over $15,720 per year. If you go over that amount, there is a one-dollar fine for every two dollars you earn. That's half.

For instance if you are 62, collecting Social Security payments and earn $30,720 in a year, you will have earned $15,000 over the limit. Your penalty would be $7,500.

It's important to note that the penalty is not assessed at the time you earn it, but after you file your tax return. It is then deducted from your monthly Social Security payment. Your payment will be withheld until the penalty is satisfied. If you owe $7,500 and your monthly payment is $1,500, You will not receive a Social Security check for *five* months sometime in the future. Don't get caught by surprise. Calculate for this in your budget.

If you plan on working full-time and making more than $15,720, you may want to wait until your FRA to apply for Social Security benefits. This is a big consideration when deciding when to begin collecting.

The penalty and maximum you can earn change in the year of your FRA. The amount you can earn before you are penalized is $41,880. If you make more than that, the penalty is $1 for every $3 you earn. If you have been penalized for earning over the allowed limit, once you reach FRA, your benefit will be recalculated with those months included and will result in an increase in your monthly payment.

If you have earned more in any recent year than in one of your previous 35 years, Social Security will recalculate your benefit automatically. It will replace a past lower earning year with a current higher earning year, thereby increasing your monthly payment. Once you reach your FRA, there is no limit to the amount you can earn without penalty. This is true for the rest of your life. It's important to note that even though you can begin collecting Social Security at 62, Medicare doesn't start until age 65. If you are no longer working full-time and your health insurance was through your employer, you'll need to find an alternate source of coverage.

Taxes

Federal
Social Security benefits are considered income by the Internal Revenue Service and are subject to Federal tax. The tax rate depends on your total income and tax bracket. If your payment is at or near the minimum, it is unlikely you will need to pay tax. If you have a higher payment and/or additional income, you may have to pay tax on a portion of your Social Security income. You will never need to pay tax on more than 85% of your benefit.

State
Several states do not have income tax: Texas, Wyoming, Alaska, Florida, Nevada, South Dakota, and Washington. New Hampshire and Tennessee have a tax on dividend and interest income only. In these nine states, Social Security payments will not be subject to state income tax, which makes them attractive to retirees on a budget. Each other state will have its own tax rate.

Payroll Tax
Often people inquire, "When will they stop taking Social Security tax out of my paycheck?" Believe it or not, as long as you are earning money, you are required to pay Social Security tax. This applies even if you are collecting Social Security and are past your FRA. Payroll tax never ends.

What if You Are Married?

In most married couples today, both individuals have earned enough on their own record to be eligible for Social Security. Benefits on your own record are paid at 100% at FRA, whereas payments on your spouse's record are paid at 50%. With the new rules, when you file it will be considered you are filing for both and you will receive the higher of the two.

The rules and regulations previously used by married couples to maximize their benefits have recently changed. The Bipartisan Budget Act of 2015 was signed into law on November 2, 2015, and significant changes in Social Security rules and regulations will result.

The two most important changes are:

- The file and suspend strategy.
- The claim and switch.

The File and Suspend

Previously one wage earner in a couple would file for benefits at FRA. Filing makes their spouse eligible to begin collecting spousal benefits. The primary wage earner could then suspend receiving payments, which allows their future benefit amount to continue to increase 8% per year until age 70. This would provide the maximum monthly amount for the remainder of their life. At the same time, the spouse is collecting spousal benefits, which could amount to as much as $63,000 over those four years.

Under the new rule, you can still suspend and get the increase, but you must be collecting payments in order for your spouse to receive spousal support. If you suspend your payment, you also suspend theirs. (This applies to all individuals eligible to collect on your work record—spouse, ex-spouse, dependent children, the disabled, and others.)

An eligible spouse receives 50% of the primary earner's benefit. This does not decrease the primary wage earner's benefit. It is in addition to. If the spouse has not yet reached FRA, they will receive a reduced amount. In the past a spouse could receive 50% of the primary earner's benefit while the primary earner's benefit continued to increase. Now, a couple gets one or the other. They can wait and get the 8% per year increase on the primary earner's benefit eliminating spousal support, or they can both begin collecting benefits.

The Restricted Application

In relation to the file and suspend strategy, the person collecting spousal support at FRA was able to allow their own benefit to increase the 8% per year while at the same time collecting spousal support. At age 70 this individual would switch from receiving spousal benefits to receiving benefits on their own record, which would now have increased by 32% and reached the maximum amount. These higher payments would be paid for the remainder of their life.

If you currently have filed and suspended or are collecting benefits on another person's record you are grandfathered in and will not lose your benefits. The law allows a six month grace period (180 days from the signing of the law, *remember it's a leap year*) for you to file and suspend if you will turn 66 within that time period.

- If you were born before April 30, 1950, you are able to file and suspend in the next 180 days and release benefits for others eligible to receive payment on your work record.
- If you were born after April 30, 1950, you are able to file and suspend, but by suspending you will suspend all benefits payable on your work record.

The new rule says that if you suspend your benefits, you suspend all benefits related to your account. Likewise, if you are receiving payments, you allow your spouse and others eligible to receive benefits, too.

The Claim and Switch

- If you were born before December 31, 1953, (age 62 in 2015) you may still file for spousal support at age 66 (four years from now) and then switch to your own benefit at age 70.

- If you were born after December 31, 1953 when you apply for benefits, you will get the higher of your benefit and spousal benefit, but not both. Once you receive benefits from one account, you cannot change to the other.

If you have not reached your FRA, you will get the higher of the two benefits you are entitled to at a decreased percentage. Keep in mind that when one person of a couple passes away, the remaining partner receives one, not two, monthly Social Security payments. It will be the higher of the two payments.

It may be beneficial to maximize the primary earner's payment by waiting as long as possible to collect so that when one spouse dies, the remaining partner has the highest payment possible when receiving only one check. Survivor benefits are paid at 100%.

Women generally live longer than men, and this can be a great financial burden at a difficult time in life. Not only does one lose a partner, but also a significant portion of income. This is when many elderly women fall below the poverty level.

Deciding when to apply and collect Social Security benefits can be a complicated decision. There are many factors and a lot at stake. Your financial situation, employment choices, assets, tax brackets, health, and expected Social Security payment amounts, must be considered. Because of the new rules, your decision is more crucial than ever. Once you commit, there's no going back.

The Basic Rules of Spousal Support

With Spousal Support, one spouse is able to collect 50% of the amount of the other's payment. This does not decrease the first spouse's payment. It is in addition to. A couple is able to collect 150% of the major wage earner's benefit. To collect spousal support:

- You must be at least 62 years of age.
- Your spouse must have filed for and be receiving retirement benefits. Benefits cannot be suspended.
- You must have been married for at least one year.
- Only one individual of a married couple can collect Spousal Support.

If you are married and have enough retirement credits on your own record and have reached FRA, you can suspend your own benefit and allow it to increase until age 70. You may not collect spousal support during this time.

- At age 70, when your benefit has reached its maximum you can begin collecting 100% plus the additional 32% earned in Delayed Retirement Credits. This ensures you will receive the highest monthly payment on your own record from age 70 onward.

- If the amount you would receive on your own record is less than what you would receive in spousal support, you will receive spousal support from that point forward.
- If you have not reached your FRA and do not have enough credits on your own record to collect benefits, you may begin collecting spousal support at age 62. However, your monthly benefit will be decreased up to 30%. This is the amount you will receive for life.
- If you have not reached FRA and the amount you would receive on your own record is higher than what you would receive in spousal benefits, you will collect on your own record and are not eligible for spousal benefits.

You can collect only one monthly check from Social Security, not both. Therefore, it is important to consider your situation wisely. These decisions are permanent and affect your income from the time you apply forward.

Can I Collect Spousal Support If I Am Divorced?

Yes you can, but there are different criteria than for a married individual.

- You must have been married for at least 10 years.
- You must be unmarried.
- You must be divorced two years or more.
- You must be at least 62.
- Your former spouse must be at least 62.
- Unlike married couples, both divorced partners can collect benefits on each other's record.
- The maximum amount of your benefit is 50% of your former spouse's payment at the time you apply for benefits. Under the old rule, the ex-spouse would not have had to apply for benefits for you to be able to collect on their record. Under the new rule, they would. This could present a problem for ex-spouses who are not on good terms.
- Your award does not affect your spouse's at all. Nor does it affect the benefits of a current spouse.

Because of privacy laws, Social Security cannot give out information regarding your spouse's record or whether or not they have applied for benefits. They can only reveal a limited amount of information.

Same-Sex Couples

Individuals in a same-sex marriage or legal union are entitled to the same benefits as heterosexual couples. If you are married, divorced, or a survivor of a same-sex couple, it is recommended that you check with the Social Security Administration to see what benefit you may be entitled to.

Survivor Benefits—What if Your Spouse is Deceased?

Social Security provides Survivor Benefits to the family of a deceased worker who has contributed to the system and is eligible for benefits. Spousal Survivor benefits are paid at 100% of the worker's entitled amount. The payment amount is determined by the contributions of the worker and the age at which he or she died.

- The surviving spouse may apply for benefits at age 60, but will receive a reduced rate for collecting early. When applying at FRA, the surviving spouse will receive 100% of the benefit.
- If the surviving spouse remarries before the age of 60, they are no longer entitled to the Survivor Benefit on the previous spouse. If the surviving spouse marries after the age of 60, they are able to receive the benefit as long as they live.

- A surviving divorced spouse may be entitled to benefits if they were married for at least 10 years and did not remarry before age 60. If they remarry after age 60, they are still able to receive full Survivor Benefits for the rest of their lives or until they switch to their own benefit if eligible.
- Although a divorced spouse can apply at age 60, if you do so before your FRA, your monthly payment amount will be reduced accordingly.
- Surviving spouses and children are entitled to a one-time benefit of $255. Other survivors are not.

How Can You Apply?

You can apply for Social Security benefits online, in person, or over the phone.

Online

To apply online, go to SSA.gov and open a "My Social Security" account. If you are over 62, you will have access to the application. The application takes about 15–30 minutes to complete. Before you begin filling out the application, it is recommended you know the following:

- your FRA,
- the consequences of applying early,

- if you will work and how much you can earn without penalty,
- your approximate life expectancy, as much as you are able.

You don't have to fill out the application at one sitting. You can leave it and come back to it later. The application is not available 24 hours a day. Check availability in advance.

By Phone
Call 1-800-772-1213. You will be connected to a recording and choose to hold or get a call back at a specified time. You can then make a specific appointment to complete your application with an agent.

In Person
You can find the nearest Social Security location online or from the main number 1-800-772-1213. You can then make an appointment to have an agent assist you in filling out your application.

Windfall Elimination Provision-Does this apply to you?

If you are eligible for a government pension—firefighters, police officers, teachers, and others—and *have not* contributed to Social Security while working at *that* job, and worked at another job at another point in time where you did contribute to

Social Security, you may be subject to the Windfall Elimination Provision.

If you have worked at another job and paid into Social Security and earned at least 40 credits, you are eligible for benefits, but your expected monthly Social Security payment may be reduced significantly. Here's why:

Social Security calculates your benefits by taking your 35 highest earning years. Any years you did not contribute are calculated as zero. Because you have many years during which you didn't pay Social Security tax, the total amount you contributed over your working lifetime will be low and it will appear that you are a low income worker when you are not. As part of the Social Security formula used to calculate your monthly benefit, lower income individuals receive a higher percentage of their contributions. This means that the government worker's monthly payment will be calculated at a higher rate than it should because these workers have been contributing to a pension fund and are not actually low income.

Windfall Elimination prevents government workers from collecting their full pension and a full Social Security benefit. The Social Security benefit is recalculated using the proper income level, which lowers the payment. The real problem here is not the policy, it's that many government workers are not aware of it and don't take it into account when calculating their retirement income. It can be devastating to learn about this regulation at a late date when you haven't planned for it. Windfall

Elimination can decrease your Social Security payment by about two thirds.

There are many government positions where employees *do* pay into Social Security. The Windfall Elimination Provision would not apply to those.

Government Pension Offset

The Government Pension Offset is similar to the Windfall Elimination Provision in that your Social Security benefit may be reduced.

If you worked in a government job and paid into a pension and did not pay into Social Security, when your spouse dies, you do not receive both your pension and your spouse's full Social Security benefit. Social Security will deduct two-thirds of your pension amount from your Survivor benefit.

The logic behind this regulation is that if two individuals of a married couple both worked in the private sector and contributed to Social Security when one passes away the survivor is entitled to only one benefit. They will receive either benefits calculated on their own record or benefits calculated on their spouse's record. They get the higher of the two. They lose one benefit entirely.

The Government Pension Offset is modeled on that Social Security regulation. It is to ensure there is some parity between the two systems and to make sure no one is receiving two full benefits at one time.

A problem with both the Windfall Elimination Provision and the Government Pension Offset is that many workers are not aware of them and they overestimate their retirement income. This can have grave consequences on the financial status and retirement lifestyle of the surviving spouse.

Can You Collect Social Security While Living Abroad?

Absolutely! You can collect Social Security payments just about anywhere in the world except North Korea or Cuba. With electronic banking and International Direct Deposit, receiving your benefits abroad has become much easier. The U.S. has various treaties with numerous countries. It's always good to verify the circumstances and procedures for receiving Social Security payments in any nation you plan to live.

Social Security works. It is the most successful and popular program we have. It's a great asset to the American people. It's comforting to know that income will be provided to you and your family when you need it most.

Medicare

Medicare is the national health insurance plan for workers in the United States age 65 or older. You pay into the plan with payroll taxes. A small portion of your earnings, 1.45%, are deducted from each of your paychecks. Your employer matches that amount for a total contribution of 2.9% in your name. There is no cap to Medicare tax. You pay tax on your total earnings no matter how high.

Unlike Social Security, which is totally autonomous and not part of the national budget or deficit, Medicare is subsidized. Part A is paid for entirely by tax revenues. Part B and D are paid for by premiums and Federal subsidies.

To qualify for Medicare, you must have been a legal resident of the United States for five consecutive years, have earned 40 Social Security credits, and paid Medicare tax for at least 10 years. If you qualify for Social Security retirement benefits, you will qualify for Medicare. Spouses, ex-spouses, and widows of eligible workers may be covered as well. Illegal aliens do not qualify for or receive Medicare benefits.

Eligibility Requirements for Medicare

- You must be 65 or older.
- You must be a U.S. citizen or legal resident.
- You must have lived in the U.S. for at least five consecutive years.
- You must have worked for at least 10 years and earned 40 Social Security credits.

You have paid for Medicare with a portion of your paycheck your entire working life. Medicare is not public assistance. It is not welfare or Medicaid. You have contributed your money into a program to ensure you have health care as you age.

It's important to know that although you can begin collecting Social Security at age 62, Medicare coverage begins at 65. If you choose to receive Social Security before your 65th birthday, you will need another source of medical insurance until then. This can be a major factor when deciding when to start collecting Social Security.

If you are eligible for Social Security, you should receive your Medicare card in the mail three months before your 65th birthday. This will provide coverage of Part A and Part B. Part B is optional. You will also receive information on how to reject Part B if you choose to do so. Contact Medicare if you do not receive your card.

Medicare is not free. There are premiums, deductibles, and co-pays like other insurance plans.

Medicare covers an average of 48% of your total health care expenses; therefore, 52% will be your responsibility. You can purchase supplemental (Medigap) policies that cover more of your care. There will be an additional premium. It is important to know what costs you are expected to pay and how you will pay for them before you agree to services. One third of bankruptcies by senior citizens are due to medical expenses.

Medicare is divided into different parts. Each part covers different services. This is a description of the parts of the Medicare system:

Part A

- Part A covers hospital care if you are formally admitted and require a stay longer than two nights.
- Your treatment must be medically necessary and must require in-patient care.
- There is no premium for Part A if you have been a legal resident of the U.S. for at least five years and have earned 40 Social Security credits.
- Part A has a deductible of $1,288 per benefit period.
- If you do not qualify, you may obtain coverage by paying a monthly premium of up to $411 per month.

The Part A "benefit period" is not a calendar year. It begins when you are admitted as an inpatient to a hospital, long-term care facility, or skilled nursing facility. It ends when you have not received in-patient care for 60 consecutive days. After the 60 days, a new benefit period begins and you are subject to another $1,288 deductible. You also then begin at day 1 for hospital coverage and have 60 days of care without a co-pay. You may have more than one benefit period per year.

In summary, Part A:
- Covers you for in-patient hospital care.
- Has no premium if you qualify.
- Has a $1,288 deductible per benefit period.
- May have more than one benefit period in a year and you may have to pay more than one deductible in a year.
- Does not cover emergency room care.

Hospital Care–After your deductible is met, there is no co-pay your first 60 days in a hospital. Days 61–90 there is a $322 per day co-pay. After 90 days in a benefit period, you are entitled to 60 'Lifetime Reserve Days.' These have a co-pay of $644 per day. Beyond your "Lifetime Reserve Days," the patient is responsible for all costs.

- First 60 Days: no co-pay
- 61–90 Days: $322 per day co-pay

- 60 "Lifetime Reserve Days": $644 per day co-pay

The average overnight hospital cost per day in the United States is more than $2,000. The cost per state varies widely.

Long-Term Care (not long-term care insurance) is subject to the same limitations and charges as acute care. The number of days listed above is a total of your combined stay in a hospital or other covered facility. If you have a serious condition that requires medically necessary care over a long period of time and you are expected to recover, you may be eligible for long-term care coverage.

Your deductible is per benefit period. You do not pay an additional deductible if you change facilities.

Skilled Nursing Services–Medicare Part A covers skilled nursing services provided in a "skilled nursing facility." This would include physical and occupational therapy and speech pathology services. Medication, medical supplies, and equipment needed while you are an in-patient are also covered. The first 20 days per benefit period are paid at 100% for covered services. For days 21–100 there is a charge of $161 co-pay per day. Days 101 and after are the full responsibility of the patient.

Homecare – Medicare Part A and Part B together cover homecare if your doctor has certified that you are homebound and that your treatment is medically necessary. Physical therapy, speech-language pathology, or occupational therapy may be covered. Your condition must be expected to improve within a certain period of time. The services provided must require a skilled therapist and the associated agency must be Medicare-certified. Medicare does not cover 24-hour care.

Medicare does not cover help with daily Activities of Living—eating, bathing, dressing, housework, etc. All services must be medically necessary.

Hospice is provided for patients who are terminally ill and have opted not to seek curative care. The focus is on comfort, not curing an illness. Drugs to make you more comfortable, counseling, and medically necessary supplies are covered. Most hospice services are provided in the home.

Medicare Part A will cover hospice care if your hospice doctor and regular doctor certify that you are terminally ill and have a life expectancy of six months or less. You must sign a statement saying that you are accepting palliative care instead of treatment for your illness.

Your hospice medical team must arrange for any services outside of palliative care including short-term in-patient care, medications other than for symptoms or pain relief, visits to other physicians for conditions not related to your terminal illness, and emergency care.

Hospice care can be extended past six months with recertification from your physicians.

Part B

If you are eligible for Part A, you are eligible for Part B. If you are eligible for Social Security, you will be enrolled in both Part A and Part B automatically when you reach age 65.

Part B is optional and you can reject it. If you do not accept Part B at the initial enrollment period, and sign up later, you will incur a permanent penalty. The premiums for Part B will be deducted from your monthly Social Security payment.

Part B premiums will undergo significant changes in 2016. The deductible will go up to $167 per year for all participants. The premium amounts will vary depending on your circumstances. If your Medicare premium is currently being deducted from your Social Security check, your premium remains the same at $104.90. If you are 65 and not currently collecting Social Security or you are enrolling in Medicare for the first time, and your income is less than $85,000 per year, your premium will be $121.80 plus a $3.00 service fee. The total payment will be $124.80.

2016 Monthly Premium Amounts

- **$104.90** - If you currently have your Medicare premium deducted from your Social Security payment.
- **$124.80** - All those who do not have a Medicare premium deducted from a

Social Security payment now and earn less than $85,000 per year.

If your modified adjusted gross income (MAGI) reported to the IRS in the previous two years is $85,000 or more, your premium payment will be higher.

- $85,000 to $107,000   Pays $170.50
- $107,000 to $160,000   Pays $243.60
- $160,000 to $214,000   Pays $316.70
- Above $214,000   Pays $389.80

Part B covers most doctor visits, lab tests, x-rays, outpatient procedures, and emergency room visits. It may cover medically necessary equipment and supplies such as canes, walkers, oxygen, and scooters. Medicare does not cover dental, vision, or hearing aid services. It is suggested you get approval from Medicare before purchasing any supplies or equipment. Everything must be deemed medically necessary for your specific condition. On Medicare's website you can enter the service or item in question and receive the conditions for which it will be covered by Medicare.

Part B services are generally covered at 80% with the patient being responsible for the remaining 20%. This applies to services provided by doctors who participate in Medicare. For services with non-participating physicians, you may have to pay more. Find out if your doctor participates before receiving services so that you know what your responsibility will be.

Part B covers certain preventative procedures such as but not limited to colorectal screening, bone density testing, cancer screening, diabetes screening, glaucoma tests, HIV tests, flu shots, and a yearly wellness visit.

Unlike private insurance companies, which have a limit to how much you personally pay, there is no such limit with Medicare. There is no out-of-pocket maximum. Frequent doctor visits and laboratory testing can result in high costs to the patient.

For Part B:

- You must have Part A.
- Deductible is $167 per year.
- Premium is between $104.90 and $389.80 per month.
- Covers doctor visits, lab tests, x-rays, and more.
- Co-pay is generally 20% of the cost of services.

Part C

Part C, also known as Medicare Advantage Plans, are all-inclusive plans offered by private insurance companies. They operate like an HMO or PPO and offer a network of physicians and services in a specific area. Advantage Plans include Part A, Part B, and usually prescription drug coverage (Part D). You do pay a premium for Part C in addition to your Part B premium.

You are eligible to enroll in a Part C plan if:

- You are eligible for Part A
- You are enrolled in Part B
- You live in the service area of the plan

Medicare Advantage Plans have the same coverage as *Original* Medicare and usually offer additional benefits as well. Different companies offer different policies. Medical advantage Plans offer a network of physicans and services. Most require you to have services by specific physicians at specific facilities except in an emergency. The rules and the premiums can change yearly. Different plans can charge different copays or coinsurance. You must review the plans available to you and make sure they provide the services that you need.

You can enroll in a Medicare Advantage Plan when you first sign up for Medicare or during the enrollment period from October 15 to December 7 each year.

The main virtue of the Medicare Advantage Plan is having the convenience of all of your services provided by one company with a network of interacting physicians that supervise your care, often under one roof. Your medical records are available to the different physicians as needed. It's the one-stop shopping of Medicare coverage.

You cannot be enrolled in both Medigap and a Medicare Advantage Plan. You would have one or the other.

Medigap

Medigap is also known as Medicare Supplemental Insurance. It supplements your Medicare Part A and Part B and may provide coverage for your premiums, deductibles, co-pays, and non-covered services. It fills the *Gap,* or the expenses Medicare does not cover.

Claims are submitted to Medicare Part A and Part B. Any unpaid portion is then submitted to your Medigap company, which will cover all or part of the remaining charges. There is a premium for Medigap in addition to your Part B premium. The average is about $150 per month.

Medigap can only be provided by Medicare-approved companies. The policies are standardized. There are ten types of Medigap Plans. They are named with letters from A–N. Each plan provides a different range of coverage.

Medigap plans are standardized and offer the same coverage nationwide. The coverage for Plan A in New York will be the same as the coverage for Plan A in Colorado. Though the coverage is the same, the price can vary widely. It is important to shop for the best price available in your area and make sure you are not paying more for the exact same coverage. Not all insurance companies provide each of the different plans, but they must offer Plan

Yes = the plan covers 100% of this benefit, No = the policy doesn't cover itt
% = the plan covers that percentage of this benefit. N/A = not applicable

Medigap Plans

Medigap Benefits	A	B	C	D	F	G	K	L	M	N
Part A coinsurance and hospital costs up to an additional 365 days after Medicare benefits are used up	Yes	Yes	Yes	Yes	Yes	Yes	Yes	Yes	Yes	Yes
Part B coinsurance or copayment	Yes	Yes	Yes	Yes	Yes	Yes	50%	75%	Yes	Yes***
Blood (first 3 pints)	Yes	Yes	Yes	Yes	Yes	Yes	50%	75%	Yes	Yes
Part A hospice care coinsurance or copayment	Yes	Yes	Yes	Yes	Yes	Yes	50%	75%	Yes	Yes
Skilled nursing facility care coinsurance	Yes	Yes	Yes	Yes	Yes	Yes	50%	75%	Yes	Yes
Part A deductible	No	No	Yes	Yes	Yes	Yes	50%	75%	50%	Yes
Part B deductible	No	No	Yes	No	Yes	No	No	No	No	No
Part B excess charges	No	No	No	No	Yes	Yes	No	No	No	No
Foreign travel exchange (up to plan limits)	No	No	80%	80%	80%	80%	No	No	80%	80%
Out-of-pocket limit**	N/A	N/A	N/A	N/A	N/A	N/A	$4,940	$2,470	N/A	N/A

A, C, and F, if they offer any. Massachusetts, Minnesota, and Wisconsin do not necessarily adhere to the standardized policies. The chart on the previous page is taken from the Medigap section of the Medicare website www.medicare.gov.

The average cost of a Medigap policy is $150 per month. The premium for the high-deductible Plan F on the chart is $60 per month. The initial cost of a policy may or may not be age dependent. Premiums may or may not be able to increase with time. Check your policy carefully.

If you are still working and have health insurance through your employer, your provider may or may not be an approved company. If it is not, you will not be eligible for Medicare until you discontinue that plan. Once you stop using your employer's policy, you have eight months to apply for Medicare before penalties are incurred. The penalty can be 10% of your premium and will be charged permanently. COBRA does not keep you from incurring the penalty.

Medigap or Supplemental Insurance:

- Is in addition to Part A and Part B coverage.
- May pay for premiums, deductibles and co-pays.
- Has 10 standardized policies lettered A–N
- Prices vary but average $150 per month.

- Does not cover spouses. Each individual must have his/her own policy.

Part D

- Medicare Part D is Prescription Drug Coverage.
- To qualify, you must participate in Part A and Part B. Part C, all-inclusive policies, generally include Prescription Drug Coverage.
- Medicare itself does not offer Part D policies.
- The coverage is provided by Medicare-approved insurance companies.
- Each company has the right to set prices, premiums, deductibles, co-pays, and decide which medications they cover.
- The policies must conform to certain standards, but the coverage can vary widely.

Medicare provides a Plan Finder on its website that will assist you in finding a company in your area that covers the medications you need. You enter your prescription name, dosage, and frequency. You will then get a list of companies and the cost of the premium, deductible, and co-pay required.

Beware the *gap* or infamous *donut hole* in Part D policies outlined here:

- Once you and your insurance company have paid a combined amount of $3,310 for covered drugs in the year, the percentage of your coverage decreases.
- You will pay 45% of the cost on brand name prescriptions and 65% on generic drugs until you reach a combined total of $4,850 that you and your plan have paid.
- There is also a 50% discount on brand name drugs, which is added to your out-of-pocket total.
- Once you reach $4,850, you enter the catastrophic coverage phase. Here you pay the lesser of 5% or $6.60 per prescription medication.

Fortunately, the percentage paid while in the gap is slowly being reduced. It will be 25% of both brand name and generic drugs by 2020.

The average premium per month is approximately $60. There are policies that cost as much as $300, and those that are government subsidized can cost as little as $12. People with a modified adjusted gross income above $85,000 will pay a surcharge on their policy.

Medicare has a low-income assistance program called Extra Help. Participants save an average of $3,900 per year. You will need to qualify to receive benefits from this program.

Many states offer assistance through the Medicare Savings Program (MSP). You must meet means test eligibility standards for this plan.

Medicare is a great benefit that provides health care to workers in the United States that are 65 or older and that have paid taxes into the system for a minimum of 10 years. The goal of this program is to ensure proper health care to those who have worked and contributed to our society at the time you may need it most.

Conclusion

The rules and regulations of Social Security and Medicare can be confusing and are often overwhelming. I wrote this book with the hope of clarifying some of the basic information you need to know to navigate through these systems and get the most out of the benefits you have paid for.

Because of the timing, I was able to include the recent changes to these programs made by The Bipartisan Budget Act of 2015. The new rules for Social Security and pricing for Medicare touch us all and it's important to know how they affect you.

Social Security is the most successful and well-regarded program ever instituted in the U.S. It has provided income to the elderly, disabled, widowed, and orphaned for over 80 years. It has kept millions of Americans out of poverty and destitution. Yet, there is an abundance of misleading and incorrect information that clouds the importance and need for this program. Let's clarify some of the major myths.

FACTS ABOUT SOCIAL SECURITY

- Social Security is not part of the Federal budget and it does not contribute one penny to the Federal deficit. Social Security is a fully autonomous entity funded by payroll tax, interest on investments, and income tax on Social Security benefits.

Social Security is NOT government spending. All funds come from the Social Security Administration, which is funded by your contributions.

- Social Security cannot go bankrupt. As long as people are earning money in the U.S., Social Security will have incoming funds. If no changes are made, the program will not be able to pay full benefits beginning in 2034. It will be able to pay benefits at about 80%. This is only if no action is taken to correct this situation. There is no substantial reason for this to occur.

- Social Security currently has a surplus of $2.8 trillion. It earns approximately $100 billion per year in interest. The surplus is invested in United States Treasury Bonds, which are considered to be risk-free and one of the best investments in the world.

FICTION ABOUT SOCIAL SECURITY

- "Social Security is increasing the deficit and bankrupting the nation." Social Security has nothing to do with the Federal deficit.

- "Social Security is in crisis and going bankrupt." It is not. It cannot.

- "The bonds held by Social Security have no value." Social Security has invested its surplus funds in our government by purchasing United States Treasury Bonds. They are backed by the full faith and credit of the United States Government. They are just as valid as if they were owned by China, France, you, or me. In order for the bonds to lose their value, the U.S. Government would have to be in full default.

The Social Security Administration releases a report every April with projections for the next 75 years. The report is issued so that we can plan ahead and ensure the program remains viable. We can use this information to make the needed corrections before they become problems.

With small changes by Congress, Social Security will be providing full benefits for many generations to come. The sooner the changes are in place, the better off we all will be.

Thank you for reading this book. It was written with the hope that it would make the retirement process an easier, less intimidating process for you. You now have an overview of the latest information and you can use it to get the most out of your benefits.

I wish you a very happy, satisfying retirement.

References

Social Security
Full Retirement Age
http://www.ssa.gov/retire2/retirechart.htm
Social Security Retirement Planner
http://www.ssa.gov/planners/
ssa.gov
http://www.ssa.gov/
Benefit Estimator
http://www.socialsecurity.gov/retire2/estimator.htm
Bipartisan Budget Act of 2015
https://www.socialsecurity.gov/legislation/Bipartisan%20B
udget%20Act%20Closes%20Social%20Security%20Looph
ole.pdf
Windfall Elimination Provision
http://www.socialsecurity.gov/pubs/EN-05-10045.pdf
Government Pension Offset
http://www.socialsecurity.gov/retire2/gpo.htm
Spousal Benefits
http://www.socialsecurity.gov/retire2/applying6.htm
Same-Sex Couples
https://www.socialsecurity.gov/people/same-
sexcouples/
Survivors Benefits
www.socialsecurity.gov/pubs/EN-05-10084.pdf
Online Office Locator
https://secure.ssa.gov/ICON/main.jsp#officeResults

Medicare
Medicare and You 2016
https://www.medicare.gov/medicare-and-you/medicare-
and-you.html

Costs at a Glance 2015 and 2016
https://www.medicare.gov/your-medicare-costs/costs-at-a-glance/costs-at-glance.html
Part A
http://www.medicare.gov/what-medicare-covers/part-a/what-part-a-covers.html
Part B
http://www.medicare.gov/what-medicare-covers/part-b/what-medicare-part-b-covers.html
Part C
http://www.medicare.gov/sign-up-change-plans/medicare-health-plans/medicare-advantage-plans/medicare-advantage-plans.html
Medigap
http://www.medicare.gov/supplement-other-insurance/medigap/whats-medigap.html
Plan A-N
https://www.medicare.gov/supplement-other-insurance/compare-medigap/compare-medigap.html
Companies approved by Medicare
http://www.medicare.gov/find-a-plan/questions/medigap-home.aspx
Part D
http://www.medicare.gov/part-d/
Medicare Plan Finder
http://www.medicare.gov/sign-up-change-plans/get-drug-coverage/get-drug-coverage.html

Conclusion
Ronald Reagan on Social Security
http://ow.ly/VJLRH
Debunking Social Security Myths Part 1 and 2
https://www.ssa.gov/history/InternetMyths.html
https://www.ssa.gov/history/InternetMyths2.html
Social Security Trust Funds and the Federal Budget
https://www.ssa.gov/history/BudgetTreatment.html
Social Security Cannot Go Bankrupt
http://www.forbes.com/sites/johntharvey/2014/08/14/social-security-cannot-go-bankrupt/

Is Social Security Going Broke?
http://www.foxbusiness.com/personal-finance/2015/07/23/is-social-security-really-going-broke/
Can the Trust Funds Remain Solvent
https://www.ssa.gov/oact/progdata/fundFAQ.html#&a0=7
Social Security 2015 Annual Report
https://www.ssa.gov/oact/trsum/
Special Use Securities
https://www.ssa.gov/oact/progdata/fundFAQ.html#&a0=7

31335569R00033

Made in the USA
San Bernardino, CA
07 March 2016